Woman Who E

CW00591654

WINNER OF THE NEW WELSH WRITING AWARDS 2015

People, Place & Planet:

WWF Cymru Prize for Writing on Nature and the Environment

Woman Who Brings the Rain

A memoir of Hokkaido, Japan

Eluned Gramich

New Welsh Rarebyte is the book imprint of New Welsh Review Ltd,
PO Box 170, Aberystwyth, Wales, SY23 1WZ,
www.newwelshreview.com, @newwelshreview,
Facebook.com/newelshreview
© Eluned Gramich
ISBN: 978-0-9934202-2-1

Editor: Gwen Davies
Design & typesetting: Ingleby Davies Design

New Welsh Review Ltd works with the financial support of the
Welsh Books Council & Aberystwyth University

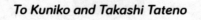

To Kuniko and Takashi Tateno

Contents

1. Mountain

The way of the valley is an immense tongue;
the form of the mountain is a body most pure.

Master Rujing

The road to Niseko runs through forest, and farmland, and forest again. The car winds around the hills, moving from dark to bright patches, and dips down into the valley. The sun, filtering through the broad, green maple leaves, plays like an old film reel across the windscreen. I catch sight of thin-limbed deer, trotting along the roadside, before slipping in between the tree trunks. Their tan-brown bodies dapple with the woods. A line from an Ainu fairytale comes back to me: *The roots,* they wrote, *of certain trees are known to turn into bears.* Perhaps certain trees also turn into deer.

My host family, the Tatenos, are sitting in the front seats. They don't seem interested in the animals, which they see every day, or the different trees, or the camellias blooming furiously in the undergrowth. Instead, when we drive into open terrain, they talk to me about the population size, building works, crops. The vast fields remind me of eastern England, where I once studied, but the vegetables here are different. Potatoes and cabbages, of course, but also edamame beans, sweet Hokkaido pumpkins, *daikon*, *nagaimo*, wasabi root. The giant greenhouses send shocks of light onto the surface of the road.

For miles and miles there is not a single house. Then

they appear – one, two, three. And then nothing again. The houses themselves are otherworldly. There is no uniformity to their architecture, no sense of style. Here is a ski chalet; there a bungalow; a villa, a shack with a roof of corrugated zinc. Tateno-San explains to me that rich Tokyoites buy up land and build their own dream homes. If he's lucky, they'll buy the land from him. His mobile rings. Tateno-San, one hand on the wheel, takes the call.

'*Dōmo*,' he says as a greeting, elongating the 'o'. This is manly speech: casual, confident and managerial. No one I know from my Japanese school would start a conversation this way. '*Dōmo*,' he says again at the end.

The welcome card the Tatenos sent me is still in my coat pocket. The card contains a basic list of information: their names (Takashi and Kuniko Tateno) and the name of their dog (Hana), their ages (64 and 62) and hobbies (golf and saké for him; books for her). The only personal touch was a line at the bottom of the page, scribbled in kanji, which I spent a long time mistranslating: 'We are so looking forward to meeting you, we could cut our throats.' They'd also enclosed a photograph of the two of them, and their dog Hana, sitting in their living room. The image showed them distracted, unsmiling, perhaps worried about the timer on the camera, or about Hana keeping still. Now they sit in front of me, their faces partially obscured, their quick speech – like all Japanese – flowing in and out of my comprehension, as if I were eavesdropping on a conversation going on in another room.

Without a word, Kuniko opens a bottle of water and brings it to her husband's lips.

'This is Niseko-chō,' he continues, after having a sip. '*Chō* is what we call an area. The town itself is further down the road.'

We turn off down a one lane road. The beginning of it is decorated with little piles of pumpkins: the lurid orange kind I'd seen in the supermarkets in Tokyo.

'They're too big to sell so we put them by the road. They're all over town,' explains Kuniko. We pass two small farmhouses. A dog – a Hokkaidan hound – barks wildly after us. We dip into another pocket of woodland and suddenly the world is muffled by the pines, maples and conifers.

When we come out the other side, I see, suddenly, a baffling, extraordinary form erupting from the farmland in front of us. A shape so startling that I'm at a loss as to what to say.

The timid repetition of the word *kirei* or 'beautiful' won't suffice. A mountain floating in the air, its outline hazy in the pale sky. Although the summit is hidden by mist, I can make out the slopes' mossy green, rolling down from the cloud for miles and miles on either side. Its triangular shape reminds me of the muscled neck of a sumo wrestler.

'What is that?' I ask.

'Yōtei-San,' Kuniko replies. 'Hokkaido's Mount Fuji.'

The colours grow clearer as we approach, like the brushstrokes of a painting. Yet the scale of the mountain seems only to increase, becoming ever more distant, impossibly high, unattainable.

'Yōtei-San,' I repeat, testing the new word.

Kuniko nods before popping a boiled sweet in her husband's mouth.

We arrive at the Tatenos' home – of whose possession Tateno-San is most proud in the world – very late in the afternoon. It's larger than any house I've ever seen in Japan. It has three floors, three bedrooms, two bathrooms, as well as a room for noodle-making and an exhibition space to house Tateno-San's considerable saké collection. The walls and floors are made of a solid, golden pine imported from Canada. A wood-burning stove lines the east-facing wall, filling the high-ceilinged rooms with a crackling warmth. The large windows let in swathes of pale northern light, generously framing the views of fields and the late-summer sky. For someone who has spent the last year locked in a concrete block, walking streets spun with electric cables like wire cocoons, the house is a revelation. Suddenly, I have the freedom to move, to stretch, to be alone; and I have the luxury of looking out of two different windows and seeing two different views. Away from the squealing commuter trains, jingles and tannoys, my mind quietens and I begin to think freely again. The rooms of my mind come to resemble the still and quiet rooms of the house. Ready to welcome new impressions and ideas.

Yōtei-San, I discover, can be seen from almost anywhere in Niseko. The kitchen window of the Tatenos' home, however, provides the perfect panorama. The mountain greets me every morning and every evening; it's the first thing I see when I leave the house and the last thing I see when I close the front door at twilight. I observe the mountain – the way it moves from shadow to light, from mist and rain to piercing clarity – and the mountain observes me, my comings and goings: its shadow darkening my path, its presence orientating my steps. The kitchen window also happens to face east. I'm reminded of the indigenous people of Hokkaido, the Ainu. For them, the east window is sacred, because it's the window which looks out towards the gods. There the Ainu offer sacrifices throughout the day. Saké and the decorative woodshavings, *inau*. Unfortunately, having my breakfast in front of this sacred window each morning, I had nothing to sacrifice to the mountain god but leftover rice grains and drops of miso soup.

The Ainu's belief that the world is peopled by many gods is a natural response to this landscape, this island wilderness of forest, marshes, mountains, bears and wolves. The Ainu gods aren't abstract deities, but strong characters with voices of their own. More Ariel and Caliban than Gaia or Mother Earth. They're even capable of telling their own stories, like the Tale of the Fox God who mistakes a beached whale for a heap of dog shit, or the Tale of the Owl God, who transforms a hut into a house of gold and jewels. Like them, Yōtei-San is a god, and as such has his own voice, his own fables. His expression changes daily, his mood dominating the surrounding district. Kuniko charts the changing seasons across his slopes. 'Can we see him today? Is he green or brown? In shadow or sunlight?' The mountain-side acts as a barometer, informing her if it will rain or not, or if the sun, peeping around his shoulder, will gift the day a blue sky. He's also a calendar for the seasons. It's the colour of his slopes which decides when it's winter, spring, summer or autumn: his summit, the closest thing to the heavens, is a few weeks ahead of the Niseko valley. A photograph taken years ago can always be dated by Yōtei-San's robe of green, red or white.

Like all the highest mountains in Japan, Yōtei is acknowledged by the appellation 'San', an address meaning something like 'Mr' or 'Mrs' in English. The mountain's original name was Ezo Fuji, Ezo being the old name for Hokkaido. It has a similar distinctive shape to Fuji – the sloping shoulders and flat, decapitated summit, like a tree stump jutting out of the ground. In the late autumn, the summit is dusted with snow, reminiscent of the iconic images of Fuji. Like Fuji, it draws tourists who stop at designated viewing areas to take photographs. It attracts walkers, too, but, compared to Fuji, the interest in climbing Yōtei-San is not great. The slopes are a sheer, constant steepness. The mountain is mostly volcanic rock, covered with moss and dock leaves, with little botanical beauty for the walker. In the winter, it's blanketed in snow. In mists or blizzards, the mountain vanishes in white cloud, so that you might never know it was there. It occasionally attracts brave off-piste skiers. A local woman I met who'd skied Yōtei told me, 'You *can* ski on him. It's possible. But I'd never do it again.'

Fuji-San is known to be a shy mountain, liable to disappear in cloud at any moment. Yet for me, it's Yōtei-San who is the more distant, the more mysterious of the two. He doesn't like to be climbed, or painted, or praised in haiku and tanka. He doesn't welcome visitors; his climate is not as warm or habitable as Fuji's. He doesn't have a *Ramen* shop or a cash machine along his paths, for instance, nor does he have water vendors waiting at the top. Yōtei-San is a different breed of mountain. A frowning, severe old man, with a face made of andesite and dacite, and a vault of angry magma trembling in his stomach. He's one of the 100 famous mountains of Japan, yet he's not among the highest. At only 1,898 metres, Yōtei-San is half the size of Mount Fuji: his brooding nature could be a short man's grumpiness.

Like Fuji, there have been paintings and poems written

about Yōtei-San, but they've been fewer and more recent. Where Fuji and its lakes were easily accessible to artists and poets wanting to escape the city, the same can't be said of Yōtei. Hokkaido, or as it was first known, the island of Ezo, is a distant exotic country: the Siberia of Japan. They built the first prison here. Men condemned to hard labour came to serve their long sentences in the inhospitable north, building the railways and working the land. Ezo was synonymous with snow and ice: a wooded tundra teeming with wolves and bears. As a result of this remoteness, its Japanese identity was only conferred upon it a hundred and fifty years ago. The central government actively pursued a policy of colonisation and migration in the 1860s when the northern island's proximity to Russia made it vulnerable to attack. In the 1870s, the population tripled, with thousands of Japanese moving north thanks to the government's financial incentives. In 1869, the country known as Ezo became 'Hokkaido'. The land was carved up according to the Japanese system of states, prefectures, districts and wards, and ascribed arbitrary Japanese place names. The names either contained, mimicked, corrupted or discarded the original Ainu toponyms.

Yōtei or 羊蹄 is just such an arbitrary label. The original

Ainu name was Makkari Nupuri or Mountain Surrounded by a River. The consonants and the quick trip of the syllables of the Ainu words suit the mountain far more than the gentler, yawning 'Yōtei'. The description embedded in the Ainu name suggests a people familiar with the mountain and its landscape. The Japanese meaning, on the other hand – *Yōtei*, 'sheep's hoof' – implies a quick survey of the area. A Japanese cartographer, perhaps, who turned up, looked up at the rock face and its peculiar shape, and described what he saw without having explored its slopes. Just as, for a long time before that, the mountain was simply known as Ezo Fuji – Hokkaido's Fuji – as if it were an inferior version of Japan's most famous mountain. An example of how Hokkaido was – and still is – defined in relation to the mainland, as if it were but a pale imitation of the true centre of culture, which resides in the capitals, Kyoto and Tokyo, hundreds of miles in the west.

Yōtei – the sheep's hoof – describes the ungulate cleft of the summit. A name bestowed by toponymists amused at the eccentricity of the mountain's shape, but not convinced of its beauty. If Hokkaido is the vulnerable, extraneous limb of the body of Japan, Yōtei is the hoof. So far removed from the heart of traditional, high Japanese culture it's hardly considered a part of the body any more. A sheep's hoof isn't made of flesh and muscle; it contains no blood or nerves. Like the human fingernail, it can be cut away. The hoof, then, is an expression of liminality, dangerously close to becoming detached, inanimate, a foreign body. Makkari Nupuri, on the other hand, doesn't contain any notions of centre or periphery. Those concepts don't enter into a language where there was no word even for Hokkaido the island. The qualities of the Ainu language mean that a word can be broken down into half-words or syllables which in themselves contain further meanings. So '*Makkari*' is a composite of '*Mak-kari*', with '*kari*' containing the sense of 'surrounding' or 'encircling' the mountain or Nupuri. The image of a river circling the mountain conjures up a kind of walking poet, a Wordsworth-like figure, who circles the mountains with his steps, and who enshrines these steps in a piece of onomastic poetry. The image is a circle – an image of wholeness, of inclusion, quite at odds with the hard, abrupt heel of 'yōtei'.

In Hokkaido, formerly Ezo, there are countless such translations and mistranslations. A huge reel of names, doubled and tripled, subtitled or dubbed over. Niseko itself is written in the Japanese syllabary katakana – a form of writing used for foreign and imported words – a testament to the fact that Niseko is Ainu, not Japanese. However, the prefecture in which Niseko is located is called Shiribeshi: a Japanese name, depicted in kanji characters. Multiple names testify to the history of the people who lived there. Like the layers of an archaeological site, each name can be dug up to reveal an older name underneath. And, like fragments of porcelain in the soil, a name, uncovered and examined, can be a clue to the region's history, its past cultures.

The Japanese name, 'sheep's hoof', reflects the region's removal from the mainland in other ways. Hokkaido is known as an agricultural country, famous for cheese and milk, foods which are not produced anywhere else in Japan. As Ann B Irish says in her book, *Hokkaido*, it's a 'non-Japanese land-scape'. Honshu, the main island, has a premium on space. Hokkaido, on the other hand, has too much. In Niseko, the farms stretch for miles and miles, crawling with high-tech harvesters and ploughs and overlaid with greenhouses. The Tatenos' house is huge because there's enough space to build it, enough freedom to move upwards and downwards and sidewards, where in Tokyo there often isn't enough space for a bed in the apartment. Next door to the Tatenos live two sisters, also enjoying an early retirement. They own a pet sheep. The sheep, fat and slow, bored by its lonely existence, lives in the garden behind their house. She trots here and there, watching me with bulbous eyes as I walk by. The neighbouring dogs bark when I come near, but the sheep stands on the gravel driveway, opposite the mountain which bears her name, wondering perhaps how she came to be there.

That first evening, we sit down to dinner at five o'clock. We eat sitting on the floor, legs stretched under the table, the television on to soften the silence of the countryside. The living room windows look out onto the one-lane road, the neighbour's vegetable garden, and, of course, Yōtei-San. Hana sits in the black armchair nearest the window, as if contemplating the mountain. (In reality, she's watching the road for fellow dogs or trespassers.) If Kuniko – the person Hana most loves in the world – goes out to the shops, Hana places her white paws on top of the armchair and scans the road nervously for her return. Kuniko loves Hana fervently too. She makes fun of neighbours who 'spoil' their pets, yet Kuniko calls Hana to her every night to check her pink mouth and stroke her paws.

'She needs to get her nails cut. She hates it. Last time they cut her nails far too short and she was in pain,' she explains. 'Isn't that right?' she adds, turning to Hana.

Hana is part Hokkaidan hound, part something else, and like all dogs, she has her peculiarities. She doesn't bark or make any noise at all. She doesn't jump, or run or lick. Her fur is entirely white, like a ghost. Kuniko is far too sensible to fuss over a dog. The things and people she loves, she loves severely, as a strict teacher loves a good student. She berates her husband for being overweight (he isn't), for eating too many sweets, for being stubborn and over-committed to his work (he is). She complains when he leaves his socks on the floor, and when his snores echo through the house at night. Despite her complaints, her husband is the centre of her life. Everything she does is for him. When he goes to work in the morning, she stays in, waiting for the phone to ring so that she can take down his messages. She prepares lunch for when he comes back. She does his laundry, keeps the house clean and presentable. They met at the communications company they both worked at in the booming seventies and eighties. Tateno-San was a senior manager and Kuniko worked in the call centre. They retired early to the countryside, as far away as possible from their urban commitments.

She's a small woman, even by Japanese standards. She tells me stories of her stay in New York as a student, and how huge everything was. The maddening enormity of the buildings, the streets, the plates of food. Sometimes, she claims, she couldn't even get onto the toilet seat. Her smallness is exaggerated by short black hair, cut in a round bob, and her round face and round glasses, buttons upon buttons. She has a restless manner, constantly getting up and sitting down; she walks fast, her legs whirring to keep up with her husband. She reads the newspaper to herself in the solitude of the late morning. To me with my half-learned Japanese, she seems curt and distant with strangers, yet always on the verge of wanting to say something, but deciding not to.

Tateno-San pulls off his socks and throws them behind the sofa. Kuniko complains. He closes his eyes and begins to snore. He's a stout man, with large blue eyes and a square, angular face which is almost western. Most of the time his expression is strained, as if his thoughts are caught up in mental arithmetic, yet he has the power to suddenly surprise those around him with bursts of energy, jumping up and running out of the house, bounding through the door, laughing at a pun. Much of his free time is spent playing golf, after which he goes to the *onsen* with his buddies. On a bad day, he goes directly to the onsen – sometimes taking me with him – to relax and let go of his worries in the hot-springs. At the *izakaya* (a kind of pub), he orders for me and Kuniko: an act expected from Japanese men. At the same time as he involves himself in local politics and community actions, he can be surprisingly reserved. Once nine o'clock strikes, he retires to bed. At a *sayonara* party the Tatenos threw for me at the end of my 'homestay', the neighbours stayed later than expected, sitting around the table downstairs, talking and drinking. Everyone was tipsy, and it didn't look like anyone was ready to leave until Tateno-San came downstairs in his blue-striped pyjamas and said goodnight.

After helping Kuniko with the dishes, and fussing over Hana some more, I retire to bed. Tateno-San is already asleep and his snores roll through the house. I can hear the sound of furniture being pushed around, a clatter of pots: Kuniko's late-night tidying. In my bedroom, there are a few prints and posters hanging on the walls. One shows Yōtei-San set alight in gold and yellow. It looks more like medieval hagiography than a modernist painting. As I look closer, I spot, right at its roots, flecks of crimson and brown paint, carelessly added. After a moment, I realise that these spots are people. The villagers of Niseko, living in its shadow.

2. Path

Autumn wind –

秋風やむしりたがりし赤い花

Red flowers she wanted

To pick.

Kobayashi Issa

We often walk together, the Tatenos, their neighbours and I, through the easy slopes and valleys of Niseko-chō. But today is different. Today we're climbing the mountain. It's a cool, bright Saturday. Kuniko gets up at six o'clock to prepare breakfast and packed lunches for our walk. The kitchen cupboards are filled with items carefully packed, wrapped and measured in plastic containers. Miso soup simmers on the stove. The rice is done; the cooker emits plumes of steam which shows white in the air. The egg alarm goes at four minutes for Kuniko; five for her husband. The housecoat is tied twice around her waist so that there's no danger of it slipping. She has already cut the pears and the persimmons for lunch. Now she rolls the freshly steamed rice in her hands, wraps the *onigiri* in nori and Cling Film, picking at the pink ginger with long cooking chopsticks.

On the fridge hangs a calendar of 旬 or shun, seasonal ingredients. Not that Kuniko needs reminding. If it's spring, which she can tell by the thawing blush on Yōtei's slopes, she knows she must buy shrimps. If it's summer, which she can tell by his placid green, Kuniko knows she has to cook the soba noodles her summer friends bring her from the capital. If it's winter, and the snow lies thick and white, then she must prepare *oden*, fish cake soup, for her husband coming back from the ski slopes. Now it's the last week of September and Kuniko is expecting a new visitor. She's expecting Autumn. Autumn demands persimmons, ginko nuts, pumpkin, udon, moon viewing. It's the time for Tateno-San to go foraging for mushrooms in the woods behind the house, surprising his wife, who doesn't know what to do with them. Every day, she observes Yōtei-San for signs of Autumn's arrival. The mountainside is like a blank page on which each month, each week and day, leaves a signature. Although the writing may change, the page remains; just as the sea remains, even as the waves rise and fall.

Already, she's pleased to see a dusting of red on the hem of his slopes.

When we arrive at the bottom of Yōtei, the weather has turned for the worse. The wind is blowing hard, the air is freezing cold, the whole atmosphere dreary with drizzle. The older women grip their walking sticks tightly in gloved hands. Tateno-San pulls his hat down over his ears and marches ahead, quickly and determinedly. In a moment, he's vanished behind the bushes, little white Hana following at his heels. Kuniko and her friend ramble together, their arms sometimes linked, sometimes not, ready to help each other up the rocky inclines. It rains lightly; a fine, wet mist. The hillside is thick with ferns, wide rubbery leaves flopping against my legs. After an hour or so, however, we come to bare slopes: nothing but gravel and spongy moss and earth underfoot. The wind batters us as we push ahead.

'Do you like it?' Tateno-San asks, when we pause to look over the valley. I say I do. 'There's a path that goes from here to the coast, to Hakodate, all the way south to the mainland. It takes four days.'

I could make out a narrow spindly path, rising and falling over the hills: not a path as much as an indent in the greenery, sailing gently towards the horizon. I dream of walking it, all the way. All the way to the sea, to the mainland, to Hiroshima in the south.

Japanese holly, rowan bushes, gaultheria, Solomon's seal, porcelain berries – the landscape is drenched in green and speckled with red. The landscape is almost Welsh in its wet, muted colour. But at the same time it's distinctly different. An American friend – a gardener and plant enthusiast – visited me in Tokyo and, in the park one day she pointed out that the bushes I passed daily on the way to work were completely new to her. She found something fascinating in their low, tortured shape. To me, the plant had simply been a hedge, but her reaction went some way towards explaining the sense of displacement I'd been feeling. Although green bushes, deciduous trees, red flowers, appeared similar to the countryside I was familiar with, the truth was it had been entirely foreign to me all along. The difference had been so subtle I hadn't noticed. It was like seeing a picture at an angle, or meeting someone for the first time and being shocked by their similarities to an old friend.

Yōtei is dotted with flowers which can only be found in high altitudes. Flowers which grow in the highlands of China and the Himalayas. Wintry plants able to weather the snow here and in Sakhalin and the disputed islands between Russia and Japan. Like gentian in the Alps, these flowers – mountain harebells and daylilies – are far from the muscular survivors you might imagine: they're fragile, gem-like. The colours blue, white, yellow: pale as glass. Many of them have the heads of bells, nodding on thin stalks. I have the urge to snap up these flowers, collect them and press them into handmade paper; seal them tightly into postcards and diaries. Keep them safe from snowfall and stormy weather. I imagine writing around their petals, letting my pen glide around the paper's creases.

We meet other walkers. A few of them running, clad in black lycra, young and old. They run up and down and up again in the time it takes us to reach the summit. Tateno-San admires them, but I find their extreme athleticism slightly unnerving. There are other groups, too. Teenage girls, dressed up for the occasion in new clothes, scrabbling up the path in gangs of four and five.

'Yama Garu,' Tateno-San explains. Mountain girls.

Hiking is currently fashionable among teenagers, and bands of friends go away for the weekend to climb mountains. They have a uniform so they can be identified as part of the Yama Garu group. Shorts over colourful leggings, socks and Doc Martens. Padded jackets in pink or purple, clutching a paraphernalia of gadgets. They walk slowly, chatting and laughing, saying again and again how cold the wind is or how steep the slope.

I'm not a Yama Garu; I'm not part of that group of young women. I walk a little behind Tateno-San and a few paces in front of Kuniko and her friend. Almost alone. I feel like a foreign element dropped from the sky. The runners glance at me over their shoulders. The girls laugh. 'Where is she from?' they ask each other under their breath. Strangers look at me, appraising me, curious to know what I'm doing here. Afterwards, safely settled in the hot springs, the women are kind enough not to stare at me as I take off my clothes and get into the pool next to them. They talk about the weather; the shift in temperature. Light rain cools on my naked shoulders. I don't know why, but the onsen is the place I feel most at home in Hokkaido. Even though I'm naked and my foreign body is bare for all to see, it's a quieter, more private place, where women get on with their own business of washing and relaxing. The Yama Garus are there too. Divested of their uniforms, they look older, more self-assured. Their faces are flushed by the steam, white towels balance prettily on their dark hair. They don't ask me where I'm from, and I'm grateful.

After the bath, we go and sit in the relaxation rooms. Tatami mats are arranged under low tables; families share pots of tea. Joining them, we open our boxes of rice balls wrapped in *nori*, and pickled plums. Tateno-San lies down in the corner and falls asleep, bursting into loud snores. The neighbour, an old, tiny woman with smiling eyes, starts to laugh. Kuniko looks more embarrassed than amused.

Then a noise that isn't Tateno-San's snoring startles us. It grows over our heads like a fly buzzing close to the ear.

'It's raining,' says Kuniko. 'Really heavy by the sound of it.'

'It's got so cold recently,' says her neighbour, agreeing. 'The rain is awful.'

We listen to it for a while, the gentle snores and the drumming rain melding together into a sleepy hum, until we're the only ones left in the tatami rooms. The sunlight dimming; the colours like the graininess of an old film. It reminds me of Ozu's *Tokyo Story*: the 1950s film takes place in traditional reed-mat rooms such as the one we're sitting in. The film was shot from waist height in order to capture the intimacy of Japanese homes. In one scene, a retired man and woman kneel side by side behind screen doors, watching the rain together, speaking about it in the mesmeric dialogue which repeats and repeats: 'Raining, isn't it? Heavy, isn't it? Raining. Still raining. How long will it be raining for? Listen to that rain.'

'Raining. Always raining,' says Kuniko. 'It sounds like it'll never stop.'

'Just listen to it! The roads will be flooded.'

'*Ame-onna*,' says Kuniko, smiling. 'Rain girl. We never had so much rain before you came. The rain follows you wherever you go.'

'Well, I'm from Wales.'

'Why, does it rain a lot where you're from?' asks the neighbour.

Tateno-San wakes up, rolls onto his back. His eyes wide open as if he's remembered something urgent.

'Can you hear that?' he exclaims.

'It's just the rain,' says Kuniko-San in her straightforward manner. 'Go back to sleep.'

I get up to stretch my legs. It's suddenly unbearably warm in the room, the heat rises to my face as if I were back in the onsen. I prop open the window, letting the cool air flow in, a dewy mist light against my skin. The sky is white but the rain has broken the low-lying cloud and sweetened the view, brightening it. I follow the road down to a point where it vanishes into the woodland; I can see the flecks of black in the sky where the birds struggle against the wind, and I see Yōtei-San, of course, made darker by the rain. It reminds me of the hem of a Kimino, a silken hem soaked in rainwater.

Kuniko-San is standing next to me. I smell her perfume. It's the same perfume that's in the bathroom at night after she's bathed. And, suddenly, I remember the bottles of perfume my mother has lined on the shelf by the window. The bottle of perfume my father gives her every Christmas; the Christmas I missed last year and will miss again this year. Suddenly, I'm scared I might cry.

'*Kōyō*,' she says, pointing at the mountain. 'Autumn colours.'

I look again, more carefully this time, and I see the red tinge to the fabric only just distinguishable against the viridian background.

'Autumn's here,' she says.

The homesickness passes. She looks up at me, her glasses on the tip of her nose. I worry she's noticed my unhappiness. But she only says, 'He'll get more beautiful than that, you know. Just you wait and see.'

3. **Kōyō**

*First the stick of encre de chine, as black as our interior night;
you rub it, moisten it slightly on a slate palette and a pot
gathers the magic juice. What more need you do now, painter
of ideas, but dip in the brush? That slender almost aerial brush
which communicates along the joints of our fingers out of our
depths up to the poem's conflagration.*

Paul Claudel

I'm twenty minutes late – no, thirty – and speeding reck-
lessly through the pitch black streets. I'm completely and
unbearably lost. My heart thumping, my eyes blur with tears;
I phone Kuniko. I fail to answer her first question: *Where are
you?* The streets, which were so familiar to me in the day, are
unrecognisable at night. I put the phone down while she's
still speaking because I can't understand the instructions
she's giving me.

Finally, I come across a group of bungalows decorated with
garages and front lawns: a suburban blip in the countryside.
I find the house I'm looking for: the garden gives it away. The
soft glow from the windows catches the leaves, illuminating
the red of a small maple near the entrance. Unlike the neighbours', the ground is covered in white gravel, finely raked,
and a considered arrangement of stones lies beneath bar-
berry shrubs. Of course, the calligraphy teacher must have
a typical Japanese garden. The scruffy western style with
flowery borders is not for him.

Despite my rushed, tearful apology, the teacher seems to
find the whole episode extremely funny. Kuniko phoned, he
explains, smiling. It's hard to find your way if you're not from
around here. I'm nodding, apologising, flushing red when

I can't unlace my shoes without having to sit down on the porch step. I apologise again – I'm so clumsy! – and wrench my boots off.

'Take your time,' he says, handing me a pair of slippers.

Taking your time, it turns out, is important in calligraphy.

A long time ago at school, I learnt that in Islam, there's no point attending prayers if you're distracted or if you're lacking in good intentions. You must be in the right frame of mind before you even enter the mosque, before washing your feet and hands, before settling down to pray. Similarly, you should be focussed and calm before you take your calligraphy brush in hand. You should be filled with good intentions. Even preparing the utensils is an act which demands concentration, a distilling of the mind.

'Take your time,' he says, when I collapse onto the *zabuton*, too tense to attempt sitting correctly with my knees folded.

Five others sit around the low tables, mostly retired men, friends of the teacher and his wife. His wife and her grown-up daughter are standing in the kitchen in their housecoats, peering through the hatch which connects the art room to the kitchen. Their laughing faces are lit under the harsh electric lights, the white tiling.

'She found it at last,' the wife says, smiling. She's looking at me, but talking to her husband.

'Tateno-San said she'd be late.'

'Didn't know the way.'

'It's so dark out now.'

In the right-hand corner of the room, a miniature wooden shrine is suspended over our heads. Pure white paper chains adorn its roof. The carved walls are covered in a film of dust.

The room is full of calligraphy. Framed and unframed; large and small, with thick and thin lines. For a moment, I'm back in Tokyo, walking around a calligraphy exhibition in the Museum of Modern Art. There I overheard groups of women admiring the pieces, chosen as part of a national competition. The exhibition hall was bare and colourless apart from the thousands of spindly black characters hanging on the walls. It seemed almost impenetrable. I couldn't appreciate the works as art because I didn't know what I was looking at. Still, I persevered, trying to learn how to look by observing others. The Japanese viewers walked slowly, spent an age examining each display, squatting on the floor to see it from one angle, moving left or right to see it from another. They spoke knowledgeably about method and materials, and the terms they used struck me as peculiar: 'energy', 'violence', 'quick', 'slow', 'peaceful', 'wild'. Although every piece was static and monochrome, people described it in terms of movement and time, reading the characters in ways I could not. Just as Japanese poets can read and write about landscape in ways which are beyond me, using a specialised language I was only starting to learn; enshrining and contracting natural phenomena into codes and beautiful kanji. Flower, bird, wind and moon: *Kachoufuugetsu* – 花鳥風月; the sun filtering through the leaves: *Komorebi* – 木漏れ日; the new green leaves of early summer: *Shinjyu* or 新樹. And even my own character trait: *ame-onna* – 雨女 – a woman who brings the rain with her wherever she goes. The more I learnt about calligraphy and poetry, the more I realised how little I'd known and how far I still had to go.

The teacher, a small retired man with a sleepy expression, sits down next to me. He prepares my things – squeezing ink onto the stone, choosing the brush, correcting my hold. Even though he's by my side, there's something so stiff and closed-up about his posture and neat appearance that it feels as though he's a hundred miles away.

'What will we draw today?' he asks me. I look at him with

such bewilderment he laughs again. He thinks I don't understand the language. 'What about Autumn?' he suggests,
speaking loudly and slowly for my benefit.

'What about confusion?' someone adds.

'Or getting lost?'

'Or being late?'

I smile. 'No,' I reply, remembering the maple tree. '*Kōyō*.
I'd like to draw *Kōyō*.'

'*Momiji*,' says the teacher gently. Japanese maple. Like the
one in your garden, I want to say, but am not brave enough.
The delicate, little thing you stubbornly cultivate even though
it doesn't grow as well here as it does in the forest. Sickly red,
speckled with brown spots, but a piece of *Kōyō* nonetheless.

His wife whistles. 'How does she know that word?' she
asks.

'Maybe they have the same word in English,' he suggests.

No, we don't, I think, but continue to smile politely. I keep
my thoughts to myself.

Kōyō or 紅葉. The first character or kanji means red, the second, leaf. *Kōyō* is roughly translated as 'when the leaves turn
red in the autumn'. It can also be read as *Momiji*, meaning

Japanese maple tree. The first character, 紅 – 'Kō' – is used in other words and can mean, variously, English tea, lipstick, rouge, russet, vermilion, pink, red. It expresses a colour so deep and broad it encompasses crimson, pink, scarlet and the colour of stewed tea all at once. The second, 葉 – 'Yō' – is one of the most common characters of Japanese script: it also happens to be one of the first I learnt to draw in calligraphy class in Tokyo. It provides the ending to place names, plant names, tea leaves, seasons, even cigars; it provides the counter (Japanese has a different counting vocabulary dependent on the type of object) for wide flat things like paper or discs, and it is used in descriptions of needles, buds and seedlings. On its own, it means, simply, 'leaf'. Most important of all is its use in *kotoba* – 言葉, meaning 'words' or 'language'. In Japanese, leaves are words, and words leaves. Language, then, is a tree of utterances; the sound falling from one's lips are leaves falling from the tree. *Kotoba* says much about the poetry of everyday Japanese, and it also shows how poetry and Autumn are inextricably connected. 'Yō' is present in the words for language and Autumn, joining them together and appealing directly to a reader's visual as well as linguistic memory.

What the philosopher Alan Watts once wrote of haiku is also true of *Kōyō*: it's a 'pebble thrown into the pool of the listener's mind, evoking associations out of the richness of his own memory.' And what richness. The russet kimono; the smell of grilled mackerel and miso broths; the viewing of the full moon. Old enka songs, nursery rhymes, the poetry learnt by heart in classrooms. Memories of holidays and daytrips taken with the family to see the maples and marvel at them. The red and yellow sweet rice cakes imprinted with leaf patterns; the smell of sweet potato, and hot burdock tea. The intricate patterns on silk cloth; and the kanji, too, bringing together language, metaphor and art. *Kōyō* is not just a natural phenomenon. It inspires a type of meditation, different from that of cherry blossom viewing. Unlike *Hanami*, *Kōyō* doesn't herald the summer months. It's respite before winter: the last piece of botanical beauty before the landscape is obliterated by snow.

There are only fifteen minutes left of the calligraphy lesson. I hurriedly get to work. Again and again, I glide my brush across the page, trying to capture *Kōyō* in a beautiful whirlwind of spontaneous action. I fail. It's awful, my attempt, like a child's. Worse than a child because at least a Japanese child knows her kanji. I can't get the order of strokes right – one, two, vertical first, or was it horizontal? Left to right or right to left? The more I rush, the messier the results.

'Take your time.' The teacher kneels down next to me and, placing his hand on mine, he steers the brush across the page. His touch is comforting, and the distance he kept from me closes a little. I try again on my own, but it's the same disaster. Disjointed and incomplete, the once-smooth lines from my teacher crumple into a heap as if trying to find some ground to stand on but failing to get a hold. The lost ink lines like dark country roads. I'm ashamed, which is odd, because I'd grown used to humiliating myself in a thousand daily ways and believed myself cured of embarrassment. The teacher reminds me to practise at home (I never do), and after he's corrected my work, he carefully rolls up the ink-stained leaves of paper and washes the brushes and ink-stone. His wife gives me a cup of barley tea before hiding in the kitchen, unsure of what to say. His daughter tries her English, but can't say anything except her name, and the name of her father, and the country where she lives.

4. **Visit**

In Niseko-chō, there is a secret population. Their houses – no bigger than sheds, half-derelict, the roof, sheets of corrugated zinc – are scattered across the valley, hidden in out-of-the way places. I could hardly believe people survived the Niseko winter in these buildings. The one nearest to Tateno-San is two hundred yards away down the hill, inhabited, I was told, by an elderly widower – once a wealthy farmer – who'd been the original landowner of the area. Kuniko, in the twenty years she'd lived there, had only seen him once when he'd had a stroke and the ambulance was called. 'They must have brought him back,' she said. 'The delivery man still comes on Wednesdays. He leaves the groceries at the back door.'

My calligraphy lesson began with a visit to one of these old, original houses. Kuniko brought me to visit a friend of hers, Yokota-San, because she had calligraphy paper and ink to spare. Nestled between a forest and a field of enormous greenhouses was a one-floor, low-roofed construction. A dog was chained up outside, its ears flat against its head. Inside, the room was filled with stuff: mostly patterned upholstery and furniture swaddled in throws, clothing, magazines. A Shinto shrine hung above the fireplace; a hob and fridge were shoved in the corner; cooking tools hung suspended from the wall. Yokota-San, a middle-aged woman with short grey hair, moved around slowly, preparing tea for us. Yokota-San was unlike any of Kuniko's other friends. She looked different, for one thing, being a large-set woman with a head and face to match. Her voice was deep and languid, as were all her actions, patient and lugubrious, as if we had all the time in the world.

Sitting on the sofa behind Yokota-San was an old lady: she said nothing when we came in and Kuniko said nothing to her. The old lady did not move nor make any noise apart from periodically patting the blanket covering her lap. Her head was bent so low as to touch her collarbone; her hair was yellowish white. During our tea, Yokota-San told me about her home – how she'd been born in the room where we were sitting, how her father had farmed the acres from here to so-and-so's land. She told me about her childhood when they'd had no running water, no electricity and no gas heater. The children went out to gather ice, thawing it for water. Everyone knew everyone back then, she said. It turned out Yokota-San had never been further than Hakodate, a city two hours away by car. She asked me how I arrived in Hokkaido and expressed surprise that there was an airport so nearby.

She'd never flown.

On receiving the paper and ink, I explained how terrible I was at calligraphy and thanked her in the exaggerated way I'd been taught at Japanese school. She didn't seem to register my words, but looked somewhere over my shoulder. She didn't talk all that much, but when she did, it was so deliberately that there seemed to be no one else in the world with more important things to say. In the silences, I could see Kuniko become restless, but it seemed Yokota-San was not to be hurried.

Suddenly the old lady, who'd been sitting behind us the entire time, thoroughly ignored, got up from the sofa. I was so surprised that I pushed my chair back and got up as if to make room for her. She seemed so old and frail I hadn't believed she could get up at all. Her back was obscenely bent so that her body was as broad as she was tall. Because this condition is so common, Japanese has a special word for this – 小柄 or *kogara* – a word depicting the shrunken frame of old women living with the belated effects of starvation in the Second World War. The blanket slid to the floor as she rose, catching on her slippered feet.

'That's my mother-in-law,' explained Yokota-San.

'How is she?' asked my host.

'Not good. I can't leave her alone. I went out for a minute the other day to feed the dog and she tried to pour tea for herself. There was boiling water all over the floor.'

Kuniko-San nodded. 'Yokota-San's mother-in-law doesn't leave the house,' she told me.

'It must be hard for her to get out and about. Such a lot of work when you're older and everything hurts,' I effused, pretending to know something about the difficulties of being old.

'It's more than that. You see, she hasn't left the house in forty years,' said Kuniko. Yokota-San nodded, but said nothing. Kuniko continued, 'Not since her husband died. And even then.'

'Oh no, it was before he died. She never liked to leave the house even then.'

'She moved in here with Yokota-San and her husband forty years ago. Yokota-San has had to look after her all this time, even after her husband, Mr Yokota, passed away. Isn't that right?'

'She doesn't have anyone else,' said Yokota-San. Her eyes focussed, suddenly adopting a whispered seriousness, she leant in, 'She's not even my own mother!' Kuniko-San just shook her head.

I packed the calligraphy tools away carefully. I was repeatedly reassured I didn't have to give them back. Once the mother-in-law was safely ensconced on the sofa again, she fell asleep.

'Wait a minute. I want to make sure she's really sleeping,' said Yokota. Only when the old woman started to snore could Yokota-San come out with us for a spin.

Kuniko drove us to the Arishima memorial, where many of the beech and maple trees had turned a tentative russet. We didn't get out of the car, but sat for a few minutes, remarking on the sombre tones and the rainclouds gathering above Takeo Arishima's head. Yokota-San pressed her forehead against the window, looking up at the statue. Arishima stood in plain view, his arms straight by his side, his expression rigid. A hundred years ago, the famous writer and poet left the literary life of Tokyo for the north country, where he fell in love with a married woman. The two of them consummated their love affair by hanging themselves in a secret location. It took over a month for them to be discovered. Now Arishima has been restored to public view, his body facing towards the forest and the tender fluttering of the branches.

'It's nice to see it,' said Yokota-San. 'I might not get the chance again.'

The best Autumn colour results from marked shifts in temperature: bright, warm days and very cold nights. Sudden changes in the climate bring about a sudden change in the leaves. *Momiji* are more startlingly red when near water or on the slopes of mountains or deep valleys: places, in other words, where the landscape is transformed in some extreme way. The phenomenon of falling leaves is due to the tree conserving energy for the winter months: the yellow and brown being the 'true' colour of the leaf when chlorophyll is no longer produced. However, the characteristic red colour of *Kōyō* as seen in Japanese maple, persimmon and cherry trees, is an exception. Its reds and purples are made of a pigment called anthocyanin, which is actively produced by the tree at the end of summer. Far from being an absence of chlorophyll, the colour is due to the unusual presence of anthocyanin. The pigment is a reflection of the tree's energy, its vitality. The last push before winter. There are several hypotheses for why a tree would waste resources on this process, including warding off insects, protecting its leaves from sunlight, or stunting nearby saplings through a chemical process called allelopathy. Yet they are all hypotheses, and there's no definitive answer. *Kōyō*, even down to its chemical processes, is a mysterious event. Perhaps it occurs simply because it's beautiful. And beauty is necessary for life. Like birds of paradise or precious stones, some things in nature are beautiful for the sake of it.

A hundred yards away from us was a small lake. The low-hanging branches of the maple trees reflected in the dark water, the reflection so clear it seemed the tree was growing upwards from the riverbed. Even the leaves' veins, the shadows on their surfaces, were visible in the water. The image as still and silent as a photograph. The experience so different from the liveliness of spring-time Tokyo, where pink petals clutter the parks and cascade messily onto the streets. *Kōyō* and *Hanami* share the same preoccupations with time's fleetingness, the ebb and tide, loss and gain, of the year. However, Autumn leaves are not as fragile as the cherry blossom, which flies off in the wind at the least provocation. They are stronger; a symbol of the toughness needed for winter, and a warning of the sudden, total change that will overwhelm the landscape of Hokkaido when the snow falls. *Hanami* is the joy of life, experienced and traumatically lost in a little over a week. *Kōyō* is about the necessity for change and the mesmerising work of metamorphosis.

Nature has the strength to change utterly. And, since human beings are a part of nature, we too have the power to change. Perhaps there was hope for Yokota-San's mother-in-law. One day, she might ask to be taken for a spin. One day, she'd see the *Kōyō* again after forty years, framing Arishima's statue. The world is constantly developing, and although there are people who withdraw into themselves, shy and frightened of life, perhaps this is a necessary part of growth, like a plant withdrawing into the soil in the winter to protect itself from the cold.

'I'd better go back,' said Yokota-San.

5. **Seal**

'Then I will chant,' he said. And he began, looking like a strange
boy spirit. 'The sun is shining – the sun is shining. That is the
Magic. The flowers are growing – the roots are stirring.
That is the Magic. Being alive is the Magic – being strong is
the Magic. The Magic is in me – the Magic is in me.
It is in me – it is in me. It's in every one of us. Magic!'
Colin's Spell, The Secret Garden.

Cherry blossoms, the cuckoo, the moon, snow: confronted with
all the manifold forms of nature, [the poet's] eyes and his ears
were filled with emptiness. When he sang of the blossoms the
blossoms were not on his mind, when he sang of the moon he did
not think of the moon. ... With a spirit like the empty sky he gives
colour to all the manifold scenes but not a trace remained [...]
Here we have the emptiness, the nothingness, of the Orient.
Yasunari Kawabata, Acceptance Speech
for the Nobel Prize for Literature, 1968.

The first book I read in Niseko – which happened to be the first English book I'd read in a long time – was *The Secret Garden*. *The Secret Garden* is a novel about transfiguration. The garden transforms from a half-dead wilderness into a paradise and, as it changes, so do the child gardeners who tend to it. The natural world is the catalyst for reflection, awakening and self-improvement, and the many changes – the blush in the children's cheeks, the energy in their limbs, the flowers in vernation – are all due to the characters' involvement with nature.

Colin's spell describes this transfigurative power as 'magic'. The root of the word 'magic' – from the Greek 'magus' – denotes the mysterious and 'heretofore unknown' powers of nature. This magic cures all ailments: ailments of the body (muscular atrophy, rheumatism), the mind (hysterics, depression) and character (selfishness, greed). In Niseko I underwent – in a less dramatic way – something like the transformation described in the book. Like the main character, Mary, I made my own secret discoveries. Like her, I explored the paths and groves and plots near where I lived, coming back in the evening tired and red-cheeked, disheveled by the outdoors. I cycled, ran, pushed through overgrown woodland paths like a child running away from her parents. My mind – emptied of its worrying – opened up to new thoughts and experiences: a feeling of expansion and freedom took hold. I went outside and saw the magic for myself and accepted it, like Mary, as medicine for the soul.

Another untranslatable word: *Degakeru*, exiting, to go out. The intransitive echoes the potential form, so that, for a student of Japanese, it sounds like 'to go out and seize the day', heavy with possibilities. On the second day of my stay, Tateno-San lent me his bike. A compact, boyish mountain bike with more gears than I knew what to do with. I wobbled down the drive before slowly making my way across the stony road, past the ostrich farm, past the neighbour's lonely sheep. I hit the top of the hill and let my bike whizz down, my scarf blowing into my face. Yōtei-San, green and serene in his summer garb, watched me travel across the fields, bridges, the ranches of Niseko-chō. As time went on, I abandoned the bike because of the cold. Instead, I took Hana for walks, taking care not to go too near the neighbour's Alsatian, who scared her. Those walks were fresh, bright, the freezing air clarifying the world around me, crystallizing my thoughts.

One morning, a month after those first bike rides and

walks in Niseko, I came downstairs to see an excited Kuniko leaning out of the east window.

'Come look!' she said. 'Do you notice anything different?'

The night before we'd had a sayonara party. Numerous dirty glasses lined the table; the living room had a weary, ruffled look. Tateno-San was lying on the sofa, his socks on the floor, dozing as if he hadn't moved for hours.

'What is it?' I asked, moving closer. Kuniko had her back to me, one hand on her hip, her face was turned away, but I could tell she was smiling.

I stopped. A gift I'd been given the previous night lay on the kitchen table, still half-embedded in torn wrapping paper. It was a small oblong box, black, with a silver clasp: the most precious thing I'd received in Japan. I smiled as memories of the evening coming back to warm me. I picked up the box and opened it. Inside was a *hanko* – a seal – with my name in kanji carved as its ensign. The characters for blessing, prosperity and sound were neatly etched into stone. The *hanko* is the signature used to settle marriage contracts, wills, rent agreements, votes, passports. The signature, which only those whose names can be written in kanji can possess. And only those who possess a signature can legitimately enter

Japanese society (vote, open bank accounts, mortgages, and so on). The *hanko* seal, then, is not just a pretty souvenir, but an official symbol of inclusion.

I read the characters again, tracing them with my fingers. 恵利音. My Welsh name, like the old Ainu toponyms, had been Japanized. In this case, it was a generous act. I was glad to be re-christened in kanji, and overjoyed that my new name could be preserved in stone. The *hanko*, despite being a slender, diminutive object, little bigger than a cigarillo, was a key to my new self, my Japanese self: a sign, safely locked in a silk-lined case, that what I'd experienced here could not be forgotten.

'Stop fiddling with that now,' said Kuniko, impatiently. 'Come and look!'

I gripped the *hanko* tightly in my right hand and joined Kuniko where she was standing by the window. The clasp dug into my palm. I thought, *I mustn't lose this.* Somewhere on the way between here and Wales, I'm sure I will lose a hundred trivial things, but I must not lose this.

'See? Look how pale he's looking!' said Kuniko.

She was talking about Yōtei-San. Snow had fallen on his summit. *Hatsuyuki* – the first snow of the year. The white lines, delicate and ornate, where the snow had fallen in the ridges of the mountain, like a lace net. The mountain seemed startled by it: a toddler who's been splashed by water, wide-eyed. I'd read somewhere that the Japanese can spend their lives 'contemplating the snow' – for the Tatenos, they had to contend with it for seven months a year, from November through to May. Whole weeks when Tateno-San would refuse to leave the ski-slopes; days when Kuniko wouldn't leave the house.

'It'll be completely white within a month. You won't recognize anywhere around here anymore. It will be completely different. A winter wonderland!'

Kuniko was right. When I visited again in January, Niseko was transformed into a different country altogether. Even the population had changed, the young skiers and snowboarders having moved in, along with the Australian adventurers with snowboards slung across their backs. I didn't know my way around anymore: each mark and milestone had been wiped out by layers of powder snow.

Only the people hadn't changed, even though their faces were half-hidden beneath furred hoods, ski-jackets and scarves. Tateno-San had sunburn from too much time spent on the slopes. The neighbour and her husband, however, were as pale as when I'd left them. The calligraphy teacher still wore his black outfits, looking older than I remembered. The jazz musician, his wife and shy thirteen-year-old daughter – whom I'd tried, in vain, to teach English – visited us, bearing steamed pumpkins. The retired headteacher and his former students visited, bringing enormous bottles of *shochu* and saké. It was a snow festival of sorts: another dinner at the Tatenos', with salted fish grilling on the hotplates, making the entire house smell of mackerel and woodsmoke. It was pitch dark outside, apart from the snow pressing against the bottom of the windows and the ghostly outline of Yōtei under the stars.

The women sat at the end of the table, near the kitchen. The students, who'd come up to stay for the season to snowboard, sat on either side of me. They spoke polite Japanese to their teacher and casual Japanese to me. Their cheeks were aglow with the fire and with the colour they'd caught from being outside all day. There was a time, not long ago, when I wouldn't have said very much, fearing to lose myself in a conversation I couldn't follow. But now, strangely, the words seemed to come easily. I asked them about their time in Niseko, and they replied with stories of adrenalin and bravado. Of a foreigner who fell and broke his board – it's impossible to break a board! – a woman who fractured three ribs; of snow in the eyes, blinding one of them as he sped at hundreds of kilometers an hour – hundreds! – down the mountain. It all seemed so simple, as if the wall that had stood between the world and my comprehension – the wall at which I clumsily translated every sentence into English before I could understand – had been demolished. A mist cleared in my mind, and I listened to the stories of the day freely, without worrying, and these stories transformed into images, narratives, excitements. The punchlines, for the first time, made sense, and I found myself laughing until I cried.

The dinner went on late. The thirteen-year-old and her parents left. And so did a few others. The students and the headteacher stayed, and so did the calligraphy teacher, even though he hadn't said much all night. Still, he accepted my offer of tea. He watched suspiciously as I added milk.

'Is that right?' he mused. I explained it was normal in Wales.

'How is Tokyo?' he asked.

'The same,' I said. 'How is your garden?'

'Oh, the garden. You can't see it now. Snow everywhere. I won't be able to do anything until the end of April, maybe not 'til May. But I'm too old for it now.'

We were sitting a little apart from the others who were busy finishing the last of the saké. I cradled the cup of tea in both hands. The calligraphy teacher copied me. It seemed so uncharacteristic of him that I smiled.

'Have you been practising?' he asked.

I shook my head. 'There's not much time. Or space.'

'Tokyo,' he said, nodding. 'Difficult place to live.'

I tried to describe my flat: the one room I lived in, the single gas hob, the futon I folded up each morning and took out each evening; one table, for everything.

'All the more reason you should practise calligraphy,' he said. 'It's important to paint, to relax, calm the mind.'

'Yes,' I said, sipping my tea.

'I used to live in Tokyo,' he went on. 'And the people there have it hard, commuting every morning, being pushed onto the crowded trains, working long hours…. No, no, it wasn't for me.'

A memory came to me: coming back from work late one evening, sitting on an almost empty train. My eyes closing with the exhaustion of Japanese. Opposite me was a young woman about my age. She was clutching a stuffed Hello Kitty toy to her chest, stroking its head, and making miaowing noises without moving her lips like a ventriloquist making the toy speak. Now and again, she rocked it from side to side in her arms like a baby.

'Is that why you moved up here?' I asked, trying to forget the woman.

'Yes, among other reasons. My wife has family here, so it seemed natural. When we lived in Tokyo, my wife didn't know anyone. She didn't go out.'

'It's hard meeting people in Tokyo,' I offered, blandly.

'She didn't go out,' he repeated. 'That's over now, thankfully. She's happy here.'

The calligraphy teacher set the tea down, undrunk.

'Do you remember your first lesson with me?'

'I remember being horribly late.'

'You were very anxious and unhappy, I thought.'

'I got lost in the dark. I didn't know where anything was.'

'You do now, don't you? Even in the snow.'

'I don't know.'

'People change all the time. Look at my wife. She's a

different person here than she was in Tokyo. People change with the times, yes, but with the place, too.'

I said nothing. He looked out of the east window. The moon illuminated the night, glancing against Yōtei's white summit.

'It's late. I'd better go back. My wife will be waiting up for me.'

The students kindly protested – Stay! Stay! Why go now that the night was just beginning? – but the calligraphy teacher shook his head, got up from where he was sitting on the floor, and made to leave. After saying his goodbyes, he turned to me at the door and said, 'Don't give up.' I wasn't sure whether he meant calligraphy or something else entirely.

Much later, when everyone had left, I went up to my old bedroom. My overnight bag lay half-opened in one corner; the duvet thick, inviting. As I got undressed, I spotted a new addition to the room. There it was. On the wall. My calligraphy. The trembling lines of the word *Kōyō* smoothed and stuck to a white frame. Each hesitation, each flaw, a memory of last Autumn. As I lay on my bed, staring up at it, remembering the night I'd got lost in the countryside, I realised that the person who painted those characters was, and was not, the same person who was reading it now.

Acknowledgements

Thanks go to the Daiwa Anglo-Japanese Foundation for giving me the opportunity to live and study in Japan; in particular, Jason James, Susan Meehan and Junko Kono. Also to the judges of the New Welsh Writing Awards, Mark Cocker and Gwen Davies, for being so generous in their comments and encouragement. Thanks, too, to all at New Welsh Review for their support, and to Ollie Bevington and Sam Christie for their beautiful film interpretation of the essay: www.newwelshreview.com/article.php?id=960. I'm also extremely grateful for the warm hospitality, companionship and kindness of those I met in Niseko, especially Ben Yamagiwa, Ellie Wyllie and, of course, the Tatenos – and their dog, Hana – without whom this could not have been written. Lastly, thank you to my parents, who are the best readers any writer could ever hope for.

Born in Haverfordwest, **Eluned Gramich** studied English at Oxford and Creative Writing at UEA, before moving to live and work in Japan on a Daiwa scholarship. Her translated collection of German short stories, *Goldfish Memory* (Monique Schwitter), was published by Parthian in April 2015. She is currently working on her first novel. *Woman Who Brings the Rain* won the New Welsh Writing Awards 2015, People, Place & Planet: WWF Cymru Prize for Writing on Nature and the Environment, in February 2015 under the title, *Scenes from a Hokkaidan Life*. newwelshwritingawards.com